Poems FOR YOUR BRAVE *Heart*

PAULA M. S. PAQUETTE, MTS, MPA

WestBow Press®
A DIVISION OF THOMAS NELSON
& ZONDERVAN

Copyright © 2017 Paula M. S. Paquette, MTS, MPA.

All rights reserved. No part of this book may be used or reproduced by any means, graphic, electronic, or mechanical, including photocopying, recording, taping or by any information storage retrieval system without the written permission of the author except in the case of brief quotations embodied in critical articles and reviews.

This book is a work of non-fiction. Unless otherwise noted, the author and the publisher make no explicit guarantees as to the accuracy of the information contained in this book and in some cases, names of people and places have been altered to protect their privacy.

WestBow Press books may be ordered through booksellers or by contacting:

WestBow Press
A Division of Thomas Nelson & Zondervan
1663 Liberty Drive
Bloomington, IN 47403
www.westbowpress.com
1 (866) 928-1240

Because of the dynamic nature of the Internet, any web addresses or links contained in this book may have changed since publication and may no longer be valid. The views expressed in this work are solely those of the author and do not necessarily reflect the views of the publisher, and the publisher hereby disclaims any responsibility for them.

Any people depicted in stock imagery provided by Thinkstock are models, and such images are being used for illustrative purposes only. Certain stock imagery © Thinkstock.

ISBN: 978-1-9736-0318-4 (sc)
ISBN: 978-1-9736-0317-7 (hc)
ISBN: 978-1-9736-0316-0 (e)

Library of Congress Control Number: 2017914999

Print information available on the last page.

WestBow Press rev. date: 09/28/2017

Dedication

To the brave heart we each have.

This life has seasons of unmitigated joy.
And times of inconsolable pain.

To keep moving forward is a testament to our true nature.

This book is dedicated to all the truly stellar people I have had the privilege of traveling with throughout this lifetime.

You have all been shining stars to me.

P.M.S.P.

Preface

It is in stillness that we find our true soul, our real strength, and our lasting happiness. In stillness, we discover our center where the past and the future intersect in the now in a most powerful way.

We are timeless and limitless beings and we connect with this in our quiet, still center. We are the seed of God placed here in creation to do good things.

To connect with our capacity to create good and to know we are completely loved by our Creator is where peace comes from.

To sit quiet and still causes healing.

In trauma or tragedy or shock, we tend to set ourselves into motion to do something, make something happen, to try to force our circumstances into changing. Rather than embarking on a mad race to try to make things be different than what they are, if we become still and receive understanding and love at our core heart level, we can find peace and grow resilience. Then, we can successfully meet our circumstances.

Life events are beyond our understanding and beyond our control. We cannot thrive if we're attached to trying to control the world around us. It's not controllable.

We can get lost in joy as much as we can get lost in sorrow. And neither will last. Joy will pass away. Sorrow will pass away. In fact, this life will not last. We are all physical beings who will leave this material world behind someday. To connect to our spirit self – which will always go on – is helpful.

Poetry can give us stillness. Poems can be sweet and lovely. Poems can shake us deeply. Poems can speak to what must be said.

To sit with a poem and to let the reading of the poem fill a quiet moment helps us see that we are eternal spirits of promise, love, kindness, and holiness.

To take a moment with a poem, we experience the holiness of this divine creation. We encounter the beautiful, the painful, the timid, and the tall.

We are not our physical circumstances. We are not the death of our loved one for we *will* see them again one day. We are not poverty, lack, hate, or injustice. We are not illness or accident. We are not sorrow or desperation. We are not mistakes. But we must overcome these things from time to time. We must regain hope.

The poems in this volume are "Poems for Your Brave Heart", little seeds of spirit that will hopefully speak to your strength and beauty and help you reconnect to the timeless love you and we all are.

In peace,
Paula Maria Salonen Paquette

An Old Antique

I am an old antique.
Solid, nicked up, wise,
But old.

I've been admired,
Moved around,
Questioned and cleaned up,
I've been used well,
And used not nicely,
Put away,
And taken back out.
I was traded,
Given away,
Discarded, no, sold,
And loved again.

But I am, still,
And an old antique.
Now valued,
Ever more.

A Cocoplum World

A black and white warbler
Enjoys a sumptuous treat,
A blue and purple cocoplum
Is fallen at its feet.

Little beak works in rhythm,
Sweet nectar in every swallow.
The plum turned inside out,
Siphoned off to the hollow.

Nature provides a natural living
To all who heed her call.
The warbler found its gift for free
As also can we all.

Candlelight

Whisper of light
Floods my imagination
With thoughts of you.
A warm soul
With a glowing heart
Piercing darkness
With a soft
Whisper of light.
The eternal whispers
To us
All
In the greatest
Dark.

Nebraska in November

The land is breathing, sighing really,
done with a season, awaiting the next.

Do we breathe, or do we just sigh
when we move from one time to the next?

As far as an eye can see,
as far as a mind can imagine,
tawny fields ready for snow,
the inevitable blanket to hide what was.

When life erodes as does too wet soil or too sick times,
a blanket of cover I covet.

And Nebraska in November.

The fields bore well.
Even squares covering the horizon, neat farm houses, breaking
in silhouette at the odd mile.

Silos, razor sharp, break the air.
Hay rolls dropped on fields like giant grains of sand scattered
by a God whose vastness we can now understand.

Nebraska in November.

A time and a place that lives and loves its season.
No misgivings, no denials, the season is.

Peace is in the steadiness.
Peace is in the acceptance.
Peace is in the rest.
Peace is in the spring that comes.

Peace is in Nebraska in November.

Fields So Fair

Around the bend
At last the gate
Which leadeth to the meadow.

A day so fair
Hath no compare
To teach the ways of heaven.

My Child Is Hurt

A parent's love
Expands mathematically
For each breath their child takes.
No limit to this love,
No way to estimate it
Or enclose it,
Or shut it down.
When my child is hurt,
I ache more than he.
When my child is hurt,
I am sick more than she.
But most hurts,
I cannot fix.
I must observe and listen only,
Watch my child get hurt.
And some hurts,
I shouldn't fix,
No matter how they pain me,
So my child will learn.
Curious set of hurts
Is this thing called parent.

Sparkle for December

Winter fell early; woods froze early.
Ground invisible, inseparable from stubborn snow.

Only spring can melt the glue that holds
the forest ransom from warmth.

Small clusters of determined leaves
peeking through the heavy snow.

Summer woods recognizable only for the contour
of what now lays covered in a diamond white blanket.

A blanket randomly tossed up in the air,
never smoothed out as it landed.

Fallen, covered, settled in for winter.

Near midnight, stepping out, breathtakingly cold, breathtakingly
still, breathtakingly bright.

Snow frozen in place.
Undisturbed crust of diamonds.

The moon's work, indeed, to give a sparkle to December.

Run the Wind

Oh too tipsy sea,
The boat too small for the waves.
Ride we must
The windy wave,
Salt our only sense.
Calm a moment ago,
Swells now to fear.
Turn, turn, you rudder,
Turn again to run the wind.
Turn again to overcome
This very tipsy sea.

Feather

Love, the equalizer
Of all men's toils.
The hardest heart
Bends to her whims.

Feather floating,
Settling on dew.
Moved again
In morning's folly.

Another landing
Notwithstanding,
Precarious perch
And moving on.

Meet Me at the Bridge

Over this brook, a bridge.
The timbers, weathered grey,
A walking way, sturdy, and,
The railings, weathered, too,
Guideposts, certain.

Forest still.
Oaks from acorns,
Maples from winged seeds,
Pines from fallen cones.
Forest floor,
Mixed up slippery brown leaves,
Pine needles sprinkled on, too.
Stones interrupting to make a point.

Meet me at the bridge.
Let's do cross together.

Colebrook River Lake

Farmington River, will I cross thee,
and will my crossing please thee?
Can I help you shore to shore, gathering more to more?
Give way, my children, to progress.
Whose progress?
Not ours, certainly.

Speckled iron red, always beckoning, safe to cross or not?
Harvey Mountain Bridge, a last testament to a village dead,
land rushed for some, bones moved for others.
Church, a place of death and birth,
built by we who longed for safety.
Destroyed by others who longed for a different kind of safety.

Who was right, will we ever know?
The ghosts won't speak a language we can understand.
They're still swimming in the river lake.

A Wedding

Groom bends his head
To kiss his bride.
Anticipation swells
In love's sweet tide.

Picture perfect,
She by his side.
Courtship complete,
This promise made.

Hope takes seat –
In this new family born.
Now, setting out,
They as one,
Love abounds.
Good life together,
No storms can hound.

But no way to tell
What earth will offer
Though heaven's glimpse
Is in that veil.

Bliss will resound and
Yield to comfort
As long as they is center
In one life together.
Not he or she,
But they –
This groom and bride,
A promise made.

Old Man Fallen

"His face fell off," clambered the news.
Dark of night, indeed it was.
Face fallen, old man down.

Granite marble, long slide down, bouncing, pouncing,
finally to the wooded floor.

Faceless Mount Cannon, facing a bare future.
Not so quickly disregarded,
face still visible in every mind's eye that ever saw
that old man on that old mountain.

Majestic face, ruggeder than a frozen tundra,
a bleating longhorn, a hammer strike on a cold anvil.
Lasting, always lasting, the face on the boldest peak,
at least in the memory of man, woman, and child.

Seen once, never forgotten.
Wish that were me.

Waiting in Shade

Intentions muted in your shade,
long shadows cast by amazing tales.

Fantastic to all who listen with rapt ear,
the shimmery wonders you claim to hold dear.

But shade it is, and shade it was,
and in your shade I wait.

Remembering the shimmery me I used to be,
to you in all your tales.

Intentions bare, I don't know where
I left my self behind.

To wait in shade, yet all in vain,
no hope to escape this mire.

Urchin of My Dreams

A sea urchin
Rambles about
The ocean floor
Safe, in all its
Spiny beauty.
Aristotle's lantern
Minds its business
And passersby mind it.
Not much
Penetrates
A thorny soul
But that which
Made it so.

Side by Side

You are the ocean tide
That shifts between teal and green
In front of my very eyes.
My sandy expanse lies next to you.
We live peacefully, side by side.
You come and go
With perfect ease,
But never really gone.
Shells dot my existence,
Little prizes between my toes.
Together, me and you,
We are the ocean and the beach,
Silver sand and cool, blue water.
The sun always finds us together,
And so does the moon.

Mountain Ahead

Flatlands subside
To the climb ahead.
Pass is narrow,
Pathway steep.

All progress is made
One step at a time.
My cowardly heart
Thinks to turn back.

Alpine Star
And Lupine beckon,
The feast
My eyes adore.

By the River

Where the river meets its bank
Is where you'll find me,
Shadowed by mammoth pines
That barely move
When the wind tests them.

Sitting on a rock
Is where you'll find me,
Watching the river
Displace itself to the sea.

An odd piece of debris,
A twig, some leaves,
Or a remnant reminding me
That humans do exist,
Float by unconcerned.

By the river is where you'll find me.
It's where I find myself, too.

So Often As We Can

With you, my friend, I laugh so well.
Belly laughs, hands on head, teared-up eyes,
can't breathe laughs.

We know each other as well as two friends do.
I showed you mine.
You showed me yours.
Troubles, of course, and hurts.

I told you mine.
You told me yours.
Hopes, of course, and dreams.

Friendships are brilliant that way, easy.
Cashmere sweaters that never pill perfect,
kittens bouncing sideways at your shoelace fun,
homemade whipped cream dolloped
on raspberry-filled layer cake special.
Kite-flying, basket-swooshing good,
Late night phone calling friend great.

Mostly that way, I'd say.
Mostly that way.

Sometimes, though, nothing.
Out of sight, out of your mind.

Who started this part-time silence, deafening?
No matter, really, just the season it is.

Friend, let's just laugh, a belly laugh,
as often as we can.

Nemesis

Come and meet my nemesis.
That thing so long opposed me.
I, beated down,
You wore the crown,
My nemesis completely.

Until one day,
It came to me
That freedom is in my heart.

Not you, not they,
Not it, not anything,
Can steal my soul from me.

My Acorn

My acorn
Cracked open
And a little
Green tree
Popped out.
Yes, it did.

Rise to Fame

Meteoric rise to fame…
What a shame,
Took so many down,
To get you that crown.

How do you dare?
Did you ever care?
Crush your friends and
Justify your ends.

What a shame,
Meteoric rise to fame…
The end will run,
With you undone.

Walking in the World

My body burns hot
These days
Feeling deeply
The tremors
Of hurt people.
Walking in the world
These days
Forces a numbness
On me
That wasn't there before.
Shaking
Like a rain-drenched dog
Helps me shake it off.
And cool me down again
To the soothing arms of you.

Watermelon

Watermelon
Takes a lot of work
And causes a lot of mess
But creates more joy
Than even that.

The color of raspberry
Blushed pink,
The sweetness of gummy bears
Gone soft.

Watermelon in the winter
Reminds us
Summer is clearly
On its way.

Honor Guard

Honor guard
Standing by
Watching.

My flag-draped self
Laying
In wait.

Why they
Guarding my honor?
Here? Now?

I left it all
On the field –
There.

That's okay.
I'm resting now,
On my back.

You couldn't be there
When I went
Down.

It's okay;
So, guard me
Now. Here.

Lucky

It's a beautiful day,
Nothing special,
But I'm alive
And pretty well
And not everyone
Is so lucky.
So I think I'll do my best
To make today a beautiful day.

Life and Death

Decisions
Don't suit me well.
Hard
To make up my mind,
Especially
About your death.
They say it's time
And that makes sense,
But decisions
Such as this
Don't suit me well at all.
That was what
You did best,
These decisions
That mean so much.

Kindness of Strangers

Time came, not a welcome time.
The day I prayed would never happen.
Happened, and in an instant.
How could it?
Disbelief.
And I must stand and even rise.
How can I?

Times as gritty as coal dust
you can never catch to wipe clean.
Time bitter times mad.
How?
Air suddenly thin; was it always this way?
Movement slow, time not cooperating.
Run. Can't.
Like the first sip of soured milk by mistake,
too hot tea, forest fire smoke.
All ruined.

Tired, I arrive.
A stranger moving toward me.
Come this way, he beckons.
How very kind.

Speaking the Truth

When the truth comes out,
You always shush me.

Never fails,
When I speak the truth,
You shush me down.

Like shushing
Makes it go away.

Well, for you,
It always does.

Shiny Gold River

Surrounding your pillow,
A shiny gold river
Of locks neatly lain out, surreal.
How does one tussle with sleep
And keep her hair so neat,
Like a river, shining, of gold.

A Friend in Deed

We have entered alone and alone we will leave.
Hoisted into time, gliding sometimes, stumbling sometimes.

Love, destruction, new life, victory.
Despair, un-care, solitude, love again.

The tide swells and rolls in.
It will not cease, no matter how we pray
to stop time or chaos,
or speed up this or that time,
or rebuild better next time.

I live to myself just as I entered,
prepared to leave just the same.

My friend, my true friend, grateful for you I am.
Just a few I call a friend.
Just a few who know, really know.

Who caused time to be still and kind
no matter what difficulty was afoot.

Those true few.
Grateful for you.
Interrupting solitude with a kindness that undoes pain.

You, so few, grateful for you.
I hope I am the same to you.

Fireflies and Butterflies

Sun glisteneth the day flier.
Moon enlightens the night flier.

Winged creatures,
Messengers of the vast.
Sparks of beauty,
A masterwork of hope for earth.

Short life on fire, short life of delight,
The sky for a playground,
Joy our destiny,
Like theirs.

Sun enlightens the day flier.
Moon glisteneth the night flyer.

Summer Picnic

Basket packed,
Summer warmth on our side.
One perfect moment
Oceanside.

Tide slides in.
Tide rolls out.
No more, no less,
Oceanside.

Living Here Without You

Morning showed up again this morning.
Night, no doubt, will re-arrive, too.
It seemed to me that time stopped,
But not so, not at all.
Not for me.

Sitting, not interested, staring at my hands,
Every movement evident, every sound complicit.

You started this long ago, now finish!
Finish with me. Finish for me.
Cold floor, dull walls.
People in various states of purification.
Various states to be.

Tap, tap, tap, whoosh, click.
Tap, tap, tap, whoosh, click.
Time spins along, marked by emptying bags of fluid.
Bag empty, full me.
Entering me, entering me with hope.
Hope for just to be. Me.

Drilling a path in my soul,
to a distant can I hope for this place.

I'm trying, as much as I can.
You said you don't want to live here without me.
I'm trying, as much as I can.
Where I am, you couldn't be.
I'm trying to get my way back.
Get my way back to you. And me.

Tap, tap, tap, whoosh, click.

So Long, So Far

So long the way back home.
Far, so far, have I traveled.

Big ships and small vessels,
Fast planes and slow trains,
Over land, through the sea,
Up a hill, deliver me.

The distance from you defines me.
The distance from you defies me.
The distance from you deafens me
To the lovely sounds of spring,
Locking me in the fall of me.

A fall from every hope that was
To the bottom of my soul,
Longing for one hand
To lift me from this place so long, so far,
So long, so far from you.

Barely Beating

Berries and a wistful branch,
Knowing soon they will be parted.
Sad like lovers undercover,
Beginning their slow walk home.

A stranger comes and picks the fruit
Off branches barely ready.
Your lover came and stole your heart
From mine now barely beating.

On earth these things collide,
In heaven, not so, we decide.
Nothing of heaven do we really know.
But everything I give it to ease the blow.

So Much So

So much so,
I love her so.
Where hollyhocks grow,
My love and I will go.

Chater's Double we will be,
Two blooms, one stem,
Us two, one heart,
We'll be.

Sea green eyes,
Solid, deep, and sure,
Froze me in a gaze,
Locked to her forevermore.

No choice have I
But to try to love
This wild and fragile nymph.
Her lips, maroon,
My hands reach to touch.
One quivering finger
Parts her soft whisper.

Where hollyhocks grow,
My love and I will go.
No other my lover will see.
Because so much so,
I love her so.
I cannot bear to live without.

Bamboo

Bamboo stretches to touch the sun.
Sun reaches warmth to meet it.
Strong, arrow straight,
Ready to be bamboo,
Beautiful wood, and smooth.
Tethered to brown earth,
Towering up, floor after floor.
Bamboo hidden shoulder behind shoulder,
Impenetrable wall of knobbed sticks,
Together, taking a stand.
Small leaves, flickering,
Clinging on here and there,
Out of place soft leaves, so vulnerable,
On stalks so hard and bare.
Bamboo, bamboo,
Stretching for all to see,
Bamboo being bamboo,
What a tree.

Civil Unrest

You frighten me.
You anger me.
You hate me.
The truth spilled out.

Into the streets,
Into the voting booths,
Onto the news,
Onto our hearts.

The truth spilled out,
And now, we bleed, or run, or shoot, or hide.
No-one is at rest.
No-one is civil.

We smile a feeble smile,
Underneath a question.
Are you civil?
Are you unrest?

How we got here,
Been a rolling boil.
Lots of scoundrels,
Perspectives, but not quite right.

Right and wrong,
Really is such a thing.
For healing to take flight,
Truth must be under wing.

Me against you, you against me,
Isn't at all where I want to be.
Blame me, steal me, deal me dirty. Stare.
Am I not welcome here?

Hidden heart is where to start.
Washington can't help us now.
Not George, or D.C., only us,
We the people, can help us now.

A Gate Pried Open

No way to tell,
What went out or what went in.
Surely some occurrence,
Possibly some grievous sin?

My steps along the path,
Timid though they be,
Certainly I plod,
To find out what encountered me.

Rodeo Star

The rodeo star is the horse,
Not he who directs those hooves.
Stout back,
Deep lungs,
Heart powerful enough
To race, dart, stop, start again,
Run, jump, and canter to the judges.
The rodeo star is the horse,
But his honor he gives to the saddler.

Feeding a Fox

Table scraps out on the lawn again,
Both of us watching for who shows up when.
Then from the forest taps a little fox,
Grey-breasted, red-backed fox, white socks.

'Shhh, shhh, hey, look, shhh," says mom,
"He's back!" Okay.
So he could be a she,
Summer, why eat here?
Good food, I guess.

"Shhh, shhh, hey, look, shhh," says mom.
What now, thinks I, above all this.
I squint and see an opossum,
Arrived to break bread with a fox.
Strange bedfellows with white socks?

Morsels disappearing,
A blissful moonlit night.
Mom in her glory,
Beholding this sight.

"Shhh, shhh, hey, look, shhh," I say.
The fox, alert, trots off.
Opossum, savvy, circles away.
The scene queerly quiet, an empty frame.

"Look at that," smiles mom.
A skunk, tail drawn, walks in. Real calm.

Places That We Fear to Go

In places that we fear to go,
We find the things that shape us.
Lessons learned, fortunes turned,
We find the things that build us.

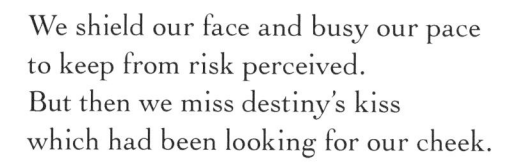

We shield our face and busy our pace
to keep from risk perceived.
But then we miss destiny's kiss
which had been looking for our cheek.

Hurry out, you frozen lout.
Don't wait; don't fear; move forward.
In the movement is the discovery,
your self just waiting for uncovery.

Time is not a friend to fear.
Fear only grows as time goes on.
Hurry out, discover of lands.
Hurry out, adventurer of places.

Those places where we feared to go,
Now laid out just before us,
One step ahead, one breath assured,
Unlock the things that bind us.

Causing Us to Care

Will anything finally cause us to care?
Or must we wait until it's too late?
Your problem, his problem, her problem, our problem,
Is my problem at the end of the day.

I am her to him.
We are them to you.
You are him to me.
She is you to them.

I am you. You are me.
All we have is we.
What I do to you, I do to me.
Let's fix it and love this amazing we.

Elsinore

Heavy-handed
Hamlet
Could not be reached
For comment.
By his hand,
The poison
Overtook
Every sane soul
And the mistakes
At Elsinore
Rolled on.
Hamlet
Could not be reached
For comment
For he fell himself, too.

34

Touch Me There

Touch me there
Where no-one else does.
Touch me there
Where no-one else can.

Love me then
When no-one else does.
Love me then
When no-one else can.

Find me when
Since no-one else does.
Find me when
Since no-one else can.

See me here
As no-one else does.
See me here
As no-one else can.

Touch me.
Love me.
Find me.
See me.

In you, I am.

Little Lady, Little Man

Little baby sitting on daddy's knees,
This little lady, every possibility she sees.

Little baby, laying on mommy's lap,
My little man, where will you wander on this great map?

Every mother, every father,
No matter where they're from,
No matter where they've been,
Recognize this seed of infinite possibility.

Parade

Rag-tag militia
Marches by,
Following clowns
Throwing candy.
Children
Running to the street
And back
To watchful parents,
So grateful
For the parade.
Princess waving
From a convertible
And oompah music
Following that.
Oh how everyone
Loves a parade.
Everyone loves
A good parade.

A Way to Go

Yes or no,
Right or left,
Which way should I go?

Stay in place,
Make a move,
What results could I show?

Take a breath.
Close my eyes.
The answer's waiting there.

In silence still,
I know thy will,
God worked it out all ready.

Doubt

I doubt
I will doubt
Any longer.

Doubt
Comes from
Others,
Not from
Our own heart.

I doubt
I will doubt
Any longer.

Keep telling myself that,
You'll see.

It Got Too Heavy

I had to put it down
After a while.
It simply got too heavy,
And complicated,
To keep holding on.

Might would not win,
And right hasn't emerged yet.

Your weight
And vast expanse,
Casting a shadow
Over my life.
Need to sit down
And give me a rest.

Freedom is in letting go
Of that which
Is that story.
That story is not me;
I choose to be free.

Of you
And you and me.

Tango In It

Everyone has a turn,
What to do, up to me.
Dance floor calls.
Crowd makes room.
Wicked tango starts.

Bodies erect,
Hands to the sky,
Faces forward, eye to eye.
One step,
Clap!
Eyes alight.

Hold me up as we spin around.
Keep me safe from the sound.
Your steady hand lies on my back.

Hips fallen together,
Moving in rhythm,
Step by step, across the span.

In an instant, I near the floor.
You rescue me out once more.

And the dance goes on,
Me and you, always we.

Final moves,
Together we turn.
Faster and faster,
Apart, together,
Starting, stopping,
Clapping, clomping.

Laughing and tears,
We become the tango.

That tangled
Tango of life.

Downstream

Murky deep,
Bottom not visible.
Squint harder,
Strain to see.
Soot grey skeletal leaves,
Broken twigs
Slowly follow the green current
Downstream.
Puddling in front of
Riverbed rocks,
Slimy tops,
Green moss strings clinging
Here and there.
Then pushed up and over
By a pushy current.
And the journey continues.

The Table at Your Banquet

Life moves on
For the not worst hurt.
Time, every moment,
Dull and useless,
Pathetically difficult
To want to breathe
For me,
The centerpiece
Of this table of tragedy.
Many have a seat for this.
Some can't face it
And give up their places.
Someone will no doubt
Steal the head of the table seat.
Some will graze through
Just looking for crumbs.
The centerpiece,
Admired and left untouched,
Remains after the feast.
Life moves on but only
For the not worst hurt.

Scarecrow

Scarecrow guarding
Field so fallow.
Crow aimless
Circling overhead.
Who will win?

Train in the Distance

A train can clack
Over the conversation
Above.
Interrupted only
By the whistle
Of arrival.
Distance closes in.
From far to near
You push.
Train from the distance
Arrived.
Hope for the future
Realized.

Rise Again

I will not die
But rise again
Like a fine phoenix
Waiting in the mud.

I will not die
But rise again
Like a wise lotus
Looking up through the pond.

I will not die
But rise again
Like the child of God
I am.

Autumn's Leaves

Mighty oaks
And sister maples
Fleeced
By the eager wind,
Into dropping
Their glorious coats
To the ground.
Red and yellow
Sailing ships
Float easily
To a lawn
Wrapping up its green
For the season.

Sweater in the Summer

Old enough to wear
A sweater in the summer.
Pastels mostly,
Baby blue or pink.
The odd niece
Chooses lavender or yellow.
My favorite color was always black,
Over something elegant like
Nutmeg, plum, taupe, or maroon.
Lion's mane beige, rainy day grey,
Or captain's navy, yes, even navy with black.
Vermilion once in a while,
Just to shake you up
And wake you up.
Jewel tones, not so much,
But they have their place.
Now pastels
And a sweater in the summer,
Soft, just like my baby's blanket is.

Among Us

One bright star
Showed the way.
Wise men followed
To a place far away.
The star, dim in compare,
To what – who – was laying there.
A mighty journey they took
To get just one look
At God come to this earth
Showing us all our worth.

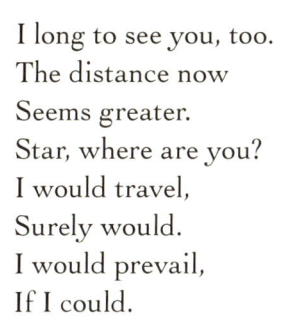

I long to see you, too.
The distance now
Seems greater.
Star, where are you?
I would travel,
Surely would.
I would prevail,
If I could.

To see God among us again.
To see perfect certainty,
Love arising, forever becoming.
The star is here, in my heart.
To follow that song is the journey's start.
I'll come to the manger, on my steed
And find that baby,
Humanity's seed.
No distance from us to Him,
Here in us He's always been.

Another Day

Dawn stacks its brightness
In bands of promise
On top of a willing horizon,
Still weighted down in clinging dark.

As time clicks on,
Stubborn dark gives way
To promise, light and hope.
Another day.

Simple Life

A simpler life
Calls me now.
Not so much
A function of age
But a function
Of fatigue
With the world
And its ways.

Disappointment

Disappointment
Sneaks up on you.
Grabs,
Forgotten bear trap
Grabs,
And hurts.

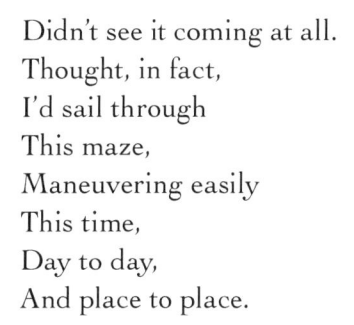

Didn't see it coming at all.
Thought, in fact,
I'd sail through
This maze,
Maneuvering easily
This time,
Day to day,
And place to place.

Disappointment
Slaps at you and laughs
Because you dared to hope.
Disappointment
Stabs,
Rusted railroad spike
Stabs,
And hurts.

Didn't see it coming.
Makes it even worse.

Move the Message to My Heart

The ground was tilled;
Now sorrow-filled.
A mission finished,
Victory won.
He died and rose,
My mind knows.
But move the message to my heart.
Let me walk through every day,
In Jesus' love I'll stay.
Until I see you once again-
The day I till no more.

Blue Jay Tale

Birds all gather
To feeders full,
Pecking out
Their territories.
Some on the feeder,
Some on the ground,
Some eating and walking,
Walking and eating,
To find their fill.
Until Blue Jay
Floats in,
Scattering all.
The blue streak,
Landing tall.

So If It Is

The day will come
When we don't have another Christmas.

So what will you do
With this one that you have?

Regret what's gone?
Aye, perhaps for a time.

Cry for what's not yet?
Hard not to, true enough.

But this Christmas is the one you have.
Another is certainly not promised.

So, if it's one to cry over,
Then cry with all you have.

If it's one to wish through,
Then wish with all you've got.

In crying and wishing,
In rejoicing and remembering,
In loving and living,
Be there now.
And be there good.
For another one, you may not have.

Dentist Music

Gotta love the dentist
For the music playing there,
Little jazzy tunes
Lifting us to where?

I know steady hands
Are essential,
But I see a pinky
Moving to the beat.

And in between
A needle, drill,
And cotton dry,
A little hum is nigh.

Nothing to Hold Onto

Falling,
Seems fast.
And nothing
On either side
To hold onto.
Can't undo
What's done.
Never works
That way.
Just gotta
Keep falling
Until I fly.

Pray to the Invisible

I pray to the invisible
To fix this pain
Permeating myself.
To fill me up
With what's already there.
Majestic, invisible you,
They say,
Ultimate atman,
Sailing along,
Full,
Observing.
Please open the door
So I can jump in and ride along,
Contented,
Unconcerned,
Invisible,
Atman.
I pray to the invisible again.

Love Does Win

Sunrise glows grey
At first
And then turns to
The pinks of promise
And finally to
The deepest blue
Of new intentions.

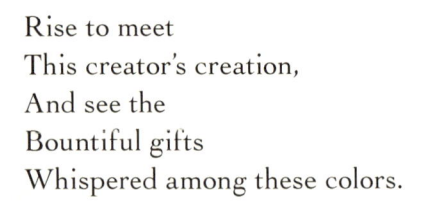

Rise to meet
This creator's creation,
And see the
Bountiful gifts
Whispered among these colors.

The air, stirred up,
Stretches to hug
All it encounters,
Birds and deer, people and bugs,
Butterflies and other creatures
Moving from night into day.

A smile and laughter
Apparent in this rising,
Love, again,
The winner of all.

Love does win
As each day turns over again
And stretches to meet the sun.
Love does win
As each heart opens again
And reaches to meet new life.

O' What a Web

Beautiful web you weave.
Invisible except morning dew
Always shines light upon it.
Revealing your plot,
So intricate.
Dainty,
But dire results.
O' what a web
You weave.

Letting You Go

My dearest friend,
How impossible it has been
To say goodbye.
My heart knows
We will meet again
But my mind tricks me
All the time
Into weeping.
My tears tell me
How much I loved you.
They water
My hope back to life.

Symphony Number 37

As I watch a little cockroach
Wander along the counter,
I realize
Just how hard it feels to breathe.

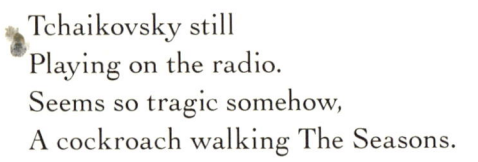

Tchaikovsky still
Playing on the radio.
Seems so tragic somehow,
A cockroach walking The Seasons.

Symphony Number 37.

Blue and Black Again

As an abuser surveys
His glorious results,
He says,
"I had no choice";
You made me do this.

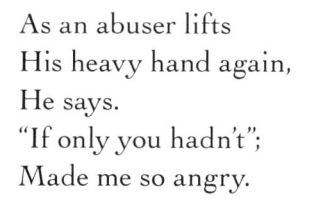

As an abuser lifts
His heavy hand again,
He says.
"If only you hadn't";
Made me so angry.

Code, heinous code,
For the battering beater,
The controlling cheater,
Making your body
Or your heart
So black and blue,
So blue and black again.

We must escape the lies.
We must not believe the why's.

Run and run far.
Shake off your shock.
Leave your rage behind, too,
For they'll never apologize
About what they've done to you.

When All Is Clear

If you ever hear
I'm not here
Anymore,
Know that I am well.

The threshold crossed,
I am not lost,
I'm found,
And finally!

Weightless, fearless,
Flying to and fro.
I see you, friend.
We'll never end.

I am found,
As you will be, too,
Some perfect day
When all is clear.

This Nebraska

Dark gives way, always accommodating dawn.

We forget, we people of stuck minds,
Dawn always arrives.

With it, promise, possibility, probability,
a maybe with a small "m",
the capital "M" becoming as time moves on.

Reality rarely matches
what our scared minds mis-anticipate.

More maybes emerge
as confidence is birthed from a trembling self.

Maybe becomes possibly and probably.
In the end, surroundings match
the reality of things hoped for.

Long roads, skinny roads.
Settled valleys, sturdy and glad to be who they are.

I become the easiness of smart, defined hills,
rolling here and there,
allowing roads to nestle in between them.

The roads we traveled under feet and under wheel
held us well for the maybe at hand.

This Nebraska, never tiring,
Welcomes all who seek refuge in its tawny soil.

This Nebraska, and the steady folks who hold it dear,
Providing welcome and a wink to settlers like me.

Mine to Yours

I am the observer.
In stillness, I seek your attention.
To bind mine to yours,
My attention to your attention.

I am the healer.
In stillness, I seek your hands.
To bind mine to yours,
My hands to your hands.

I am the lover.
In stillness, I seek your heart.
To bind mine to yours,
My heart to your heart.

And then it will all begin,
As it was from the beginning.

The Sum of All My Parts

No sooner
Do I stand
Than someone
Knocks me back.

No sooner
Do I smile
Than someone
Makes me sigh.

But, today, I know
I do rise and fly
For I am
The sum of all my parts.

I Love You Because

No grander peace could fill my soul
Than knowing you are my friend.

No distance lies from me to you,
Or you to me.
Our thoughts are intertwined.

Farewells and time
Pass all the same
As you live inside my heart.

Not clinging, dark,
But freely, light,
My joy is you and I.

A smile always fills my thought of you.
And a blanket soft and warm.
The fireplace crackling, sighs aloud.
I sweetly remember you.

I love you because,
No fussy reason why,
Just because
I love the you,
You are to me.

Marking My Life

I mark my life in only two ways.
Before you died
And after
Is how I count my days.

They tell you
Time heals all wounds.
I think I've just found a way
To spend each day
Suspended between
Thinking too much
And doing what I have to do.

Some days I think
I need to accept invitations
And other days I know
I just really can't.

I have no idea
If I like to travel.
After all,
I've never done it without you.

Where on earth could you be?
You're certainly not
Sitting here with me.
You're not on earth at all,
At least not the way you used to be.
You slipped away
When I wasn't looking.
Well, I was looking,
But you slipped away anyway.

If Wishing Could Make It So

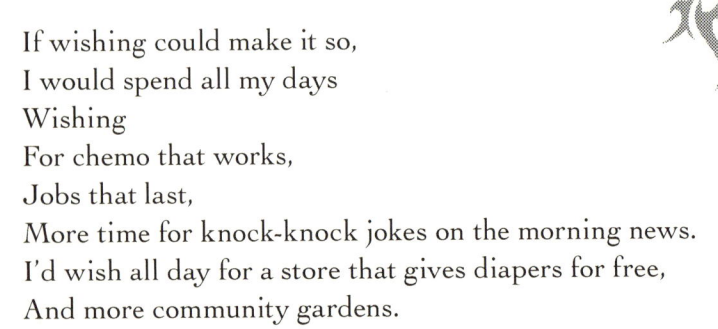

If wishing could make it so,
I would spend all my days
Wishing
For chemo that works,
Jobs that last,
More time for knock-knock jokes on the morning news.
I'd wish all day for a store that gives diapers for free,
And more community gardens.

If wishing could make it so,
I would wish all day
And try to dream wishes in my sleep.

For I wish for all the best for you
And I wish for all the best for me.

I guess if I spend all my time wishing,
Perhaps my wish will become a prayer,
Or already is.

Yes, I'll spend all my time wishing
Because wishing could make it so.

A Child's Laughter

The peal of a child's laughter,
The sweetest sound God ever made.

I shall hope to meet my Maker
Singing that sound, heaven-made.

For surely my Maker
Would recognize this little hymn,

As the sweetest love song
I could ever sing for Him.

Ice Cream Parlor

Best place on a hot summer's day,
Ice cream parlor, of course,
I would have to say.

The faces on the people walking in,
Smiling with anticipation,
An ear to ear grin.

Surveying frozen cabinets lined along the wall,
Wish I could take a spoon
And sample one and all.

Scene from the Road

As seen from the road,
Many men were walking,
Carrying various tools
To a field far away.

To do the owner's work
And seed a crop
That would feed all of them
Someday.

Men, black and white,
Some boys.

Women and girls,
Could have come along,
But not their custom.

Assembling a feast
Were the women.
And mostly giggling
Were the girls.

But a wonderful feast it will be.
As provided by the
Men, women, boys,
And even me.

Tomorrow

Tomorrow, I will listen to a bird sing,
And I will sit outside for some fresh air.
I will stare at my cat for a while,
And sit still in my chair,
For at least an hour.
I will dress up nicely,
And I will greet people I meet.
I will spend less time worrying,
And I will give myself a break.
I won't care quite so much
About who doesn't think I've done enough,
Or about who is making me mad.
For I don't have extra time today
To be anything but glad.
Glad for the people who have loved me,
Glad for home and food and drink,
Glad for air to breathe,
And breath to carry me
Through each day.
I think I'll add to my list
At least one prayer every day.
A prayer to say I thank you
For this life I have today.

The Bull on Grandmarm's Farm

Parents, keep your children safe;
There's a bull on grandmarm's farm.
Across the street, the menace sleeps.
Disturbed, awake he leaps.

At three, I thought I'd go and see
This friendly, furry wonder amazing me.
My mommy turned when I was there,
An instant gone, she knew not where.

Across the street, I skipped.
Into the pen, I slipped.
A crowd of adults came pouring after me,
Like ants out of a hive disturbed.

Suddenly, they all walked slow,
And spoke to me in voices low.
Stay calm, don't move, stay there,
They all clasping their hands in fear.

I sat me down atop this great rock.
I'd climbed it up to get a better look at the flock.
Not sure if the greater danger was
Rolling off the rock or getting pummeled by the bull.

The farmer came to pen his prize,
My mother crying and repeating why's.
Daddy rushed to pluck me from the rock,
And returned me to my mother's frock.

Relief soon gave way to chiding the child,
Not to run across the street so wild.
So, parents, keep your children safe.
There's a bull on grandmarm's farm!

Turtle

Turtle so slow
Starts
To cross the road.
When he arrives,
Where will he be?

Purple All Around

Lilac trees line the drive
To the house on Moonberry Lane.
Some black raspberry purple,
Some light whipped lavender,
Some white.
Taken together,
Purple all around,
On Moonberry Lane.

I Don't Know But I Said I Did

Sitting out in those lawn chairs,
Metal deals
With wood slats
Brown,
And appealing.

My father outside to cry
Away from us,
Away from time.

"What if I don't make it in time?" he asked little me.
"You will," I said,
But I didn't know.
Seemed all right this time,
Just to lie.

His mom had lain in a stroke
For days
Until she was discovered.
He couldn't quite accommodate
How bad that made him feel.

And now, so far away,
Could he fly there in time,
In time to see her go?
"You will," I said,
As I held his big hand.
I, just a girl, he, such a man,
Telling daddy
What I thought he needed to know.

Pretty Stone

Death has blunted me
A one-two punch,
Took me to my knees.

I kneel to
Remember you now,
At your grave.

I kneel on one knee.
When you died,
I fell to both.

Now, I'm halfway healed.

Pretty stone
I picked for you.
Speckled grey,
Granite and solid.

My name is there, too,
Although
My ending date is not.

Jamaican Bob

A Jamaican bob I do
As I walk to the reggae
Playing in the street.

I can trust this beat.
It carried me well
Through many toil and trouble.

The Cat I Loved So Much

The cat I loved so much,
I named her Blondie.
Not a blonde hair on her person,
Just a name I thought was swell.
My very faithful companion,
Always interested
When I came home,
Dog-like loyal,
But elegant like a cat.
Made it sweeter
Since cats don't do that.
The cat I loved so much,
I will always love
And she'll never be far from me
Nor me from her.
Sometimes, when souls
Get good and mixed up,
They never can be parted.

Church Today

My son took me to church today.
It's truly beautiful, I would have to say.
By his side, I'd love to stay,
But he'll need to be on his way.

Wish it happened more,
But my boy is grown up, for sure.
And his wife could certainly object,
It's her, not me, he needs to protect.

This one final time,
It's so divine.
My son took me to church, I knew.
Thank you, son, thank you.

It's You

To start my day
Thinking of you
Is a privilege.

For it's you
Who started my day
And who will end it, too.

To end my day
Thinking of you
Is a privilege.

For it's you
Who ended my day
And who will start it, too.

Your Cheek

My hand
Reaches out
And rests
On your cheek.

I feel your skin.
Strange,
How rarely
We face each other.

Sun Shines Through

The sun is shining
Through every cloud.

Just hidden for a moment
Behind this minute's
Circumstance.

The sun always shines through
Eventually.

Waiting for it
Is the hard part
But faith does see us through.

My Finnish Friends

Why can't we just
Smile and laugh about
Our cultural differences?
I find them jewels amazing.

Sometime after sunset,
You'll find my Finnish friends
Heating themselves up
In a room of 180 degrees.
That's Fahrenheit.
Sounds nicer at 82 in Celsius.
Then, you'll find my Finnish friends
Striking themselves repeatedly
With a bouquet of freshly-cut birch branches.
And then,
You'll find my Finnish friends
Going outside to lay in a snowbank –
To cool off.

It's okay to tell us we're crazy.
We already know.

Some people search for a single magpie,
Or throw oranges, the victor's gift,
Walk on grapes, point with thumbs,
And think that the tooth fairy lives on the roof.

Hookah smoke heralds story-telling time,
And the hat dance won a war.
Some brides are painted in henna,
And your bed cannot face a door.

Eat your Lentil soup on New Year's Day,
And hold your belly button when it thunders.
Walk across coins when you marry,
And set an altar to those who are gone.

The customs that we carry,
Are so beautiful and vary.
I'm glad to share this world with you,
And I hope you think so, too.

Yoga and Me

From a mountain into a cobra,
A few steps
And a triangle I will be.

A warrior or an eagle,
That no-one will ever see.

After a few certain paces,
Everyone disappears, all the faces.

Yoga and me, we are alone.
No more busy thoughts, and no more phone.
Worries push aside.
Slowly, my soul becomes untied.

Yoga wants all of you
And, magically, you subside.

The dog looks up;
The airplane flies;
The camel marches through.

Rest in the child's pose, rest.
And live to tell another day.
For yoga and me,
We are good friends,
The truest friends we'll be.

The Play in Your Head

The play in your head,
Not much to do with me.
Or truth perhaps.
Not my truth anyway.

Your truth.
That's all that matters.
To you
Anyway.

Talloires

Old city. French,
A town, really.
Bricks laid down
Became streets and walks.
Bricks stacked up
Became houses and their walls
For genteel people
Who savor life and its living.
Cafe tables outside the bakery.
Sweetest smell,
Baking pastry,
Steaming to your plate.
Butter pats and orange marmalade,
Smart coffee
In tiny cups.
I sigh.
For it's where I fell in love,
Talloires.

The Smell of a Woman's Hair

When I was a boy,
Mama would lean into me
And I'd smile in the smell of her hair.

I'm not sure what happens
When a woman's hair
Meets shampoo,
But it's magic.

Raspberry, peach,
Rose, or chamomile,
It fixes
With her hair
And is the smell of angel perfume.

Sweet raspberry wine,
Thick, dripping peach nectar,
A bed of rose petals,
Chamomile tea for a king.

The smell of a woman's hair,
Makes me know
True sweetness is,
A kind as has no compare.

If It Were

We stay alive, don't we,
Despite massive pain.
Some created for us,
That we so disdain.
And some of our own making,
That's pretty plain.

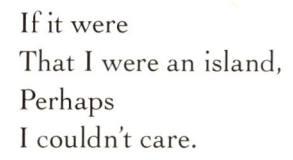

If it were
That I were an island,
Perhaps
I couldn't care.

As it were,
I'm not an island.
Care, I do
And so I cry.

But still rise tomorrow
And follow the sun
From rising to setting
That's a victory won.

To rise and try,
Perhaps rise and fly,
Through each rain,
And through every pain.

Cuckoo

In the woods,
A cuckoo sounds.
Sure-throated,
Fast-calling,
Cuckoo sound abounds.

Waiting for an answer
From the jungle deep,
The cuckoo wails
And from branch to branch
He leaps.

There is no other featherling
To answer his call.
The winds are empty;
No other cuckoo at all.

No matter
How futile the quest
Of this beautiful bird,
He continues to cuckoo,
Trying to be heard.

And, finally, as faint as can be,
A tiny cuckoo
Utters from a tree.
A companion arrived,
Greets him with glee.
Together, they cuckoo
For all the world to see.

Rebecoming Light

Between the light
That stops being light
When darkness overcomes it
And the shadow it cast
When it was still light
Lies the knowledge of this world.

Unseen place,
Waiting to be ignited again,
When light reassembles
Its essential self.

Light always reemerges.
Light always rebecomes light.

A Raising Up

I was raised up
To not blame others
But to take it upon me
To fix it up.

I was raised up
To not slice others
Behind their backs
Or in front of their faces
And to be kind
Even when I'm right.

I was raised up
To let others win sometimes
Even if I could win every time
Just so they can win, too.

I was raised up
Not to trample others under my feet.

I was raised up
To work hard.
I was raised up
To not expect anything for free.
I was raised up
That an hour means an hour
And a day is a day.
I was raised up
To treat you like I want to be treated.

I was raised up and still am.

Prayer

The power of prayer
Is mighty, indeed.
A song of essential help needed,
A winged message to be heeded.
We hope the receiver
Hears our message.
We hope the receiver
Grants our wish.
Or, hears our cry,
Fills the space,
Quiets our scream,
Parts the sea,
And dashes our enemy.
It's promised of old
That mighty Jahweh
Will hear us.
But we can't forget,
His will, not ours.
His knowledge, not ours.
For what is seen, seems obvious.
But what is unseen is glorious.
So, God,
Your will, not mine.

Bullies

Bullies are an awful breed,
Beat on others to satisfy their need.
I wonder if this terrible course
Ever causes them remorse.

The bully is mean, sometimes outright,
Sometime subtle, what a plight.
Call me at the end of the day
So, with a sleepless night, I'll pay.

Threaten me and take your fill,
Unless I bend to your will.
Pretend to hear what I need.
Then give it not one further heed.

Stack up supporters on your side
And create your victory in a swelling tide.
Tell my dearest friend a lie,
Then they're asking me, why?

You're so big, so loud, so important,
No-one sees what I could have meant.
Force me to do things your way,
And, if I don't, you'll make me pay.

And then pretend you're so right
And I'm so wrong.
All this will make you more strong.
Your whole life is a battle to win,
My whole life, just trying to fit in.

A Garden Seat

The garden seat sits empty;
You were here just yesterday.
We passed the while with so much fun,
Sitting here, in the sun.

I search the bench to see
If it will give me any clue
About where you've gone from here –
But nothing do I see.

How is it that you're here today,
Then gone so suddenly?
How can I grasp a feeble mind
Around this truth sublime?

Little Friends

Little boys and little girls
Are the purest loves of all.
Their souls
Reach to each other,
A bridge of beauty,
Brighter than the sun.
Glowing all the way to each other,
Lanterns lighting the faces of happy friends.
Giggles catch everyone around
And even dour adults
Begin to smile.
Silliness and dancing,
Tag and synchronized stepping,
Faces with tongues sticking out,
Laughter never ceasing.
Little friends,
How divine.

Woodsmoke

Woodsmoke smell
Fills the sky.
A warm hearth
Is certainly nearby.

Someone watches,
Tendrils curling.
Filled with peace,
From embers whirling.

The beauty is
That through the air,
All of its peace
The fireplace does share.

The Sense of You

Stillness fills me
With the sense of you.

The sense to know
That only you matters.

Muttering voices,
Complaints arising,
Braking and going,
Going and braking.

I make my way
Back to you.

Back to
The sense of you.

Broken with You

In the midst of brokenness,
I wonder if it will ever
Come back together.
I've been waiting
What seems like an eternity.
Is it years or months or days?
Feels like a lifetime,
That's for sure.
But, it's not.
I lived a lifetime once
That had happiness in it.
The world is filled with people
Going through a thing.
But when will my thing end?
My mind tries to grasp
How to forget the pain
But progress has been slow.
I look around for good advice.
I look around for soothing spaces.
I look around for landmarks
And milestones.
I made some progress
But, then, the next day,
I'm not so sure.
Sometimes, I wonder to myself
If even hope will ever return.
I usually bolster my spirits
With the thing called hope.
Some days, I just even can't
Remember what there is to hope for.
Sometimes, the only thing,
And that which will keep me going again today,
Is thinking maybe today
I simply need to be here for you.

Free

Someday, I will be free.
I will be with they
Who went ahead of me.

I will sing bright songs,
Joined in with
The heavenly throngs.

No pain, no worry,
All things in due course,
No hurry.

For that is heaven
From whence we came,
And to which
I will go again.

Move I Must

Genius tells me
Move I must.
I cannot afford
To stay put anymore.
I have turned
To stone
For staying stuck
So, move I must
And, move I shall.

To Myself

I shall stay to myself;
Your pain I can no longer endure.

Your pain,
I need endure no more.

My heart moved on.
I no longer doubt.
The child they made me,
I no longer live out.

What's left is seed
That these tears do water.
Growing roots
To a more fertile earth.

Roots drill down,
Ever certain,
To the place where
Flowers are caused to bloom.

So, on your way, please do go.
But leave me part of my soul.
I need a piece to seed the whole,
The whole of me returning.

Stormcloud Is the Way

Stormcloud shows
Its rising ire.
Rain to pour
Upon this mire.

Empty then
And quiet now.
Rainbow shows
What heaven knows.

Ordinary Times

We're here to live in ordinary times,
Then from ordinary times
Into those more difficult.

We're here to help others, too,
With their ordinary things
And then again in times of hurt.

We're here to beacon a message of love
Through our lives,
Ordinarily lived.

We're here to receive love from others
When our own ordinary times
Grow tough.

How well we give and
How well we receive
Make up an ordinary life well lived.

This Time, It's Me

I'm praying they are mistaken
But I think they know they're not.
Possible still,
Though too early to tell.

Doctors have been known to be wrong,
But, perhaps, this is just their way
To let us
Cling to a little hope.

So much they can do nowadays,
The family starts to utter.
But I know somehow
This is the beginning of my end.

My face has frozen
In a state of disbelief.
I'm trying to embrace
The realness of what this means.

I used to hear these things
And think,
Better he than me,
Thank God, it's not me.

But, this time, it's me.
This time, I'm caught.
Death got its grips in me.
This time, can't you see?

The Poem

The poem
Has warmed
My heart
And driven out
Ghosts of old.
It makes sense
On paper
What this life
Has done to me
And for me.
In the poem
Is the fix.
Said and done,
It's me
Who won.

The Character of Me

The only measure of me
Is what I think of me
So I think I'll make it good.

Not what they think,
Not what you said,
But solely what I think of me.

Get out and do right.
Forget what they did or didn't do.
Keep trying hard,
No matter what a target they make of you.
Take solace
In any job you think is well done.
Stay kind and honest
No matter how many steal what you've won.

Be brave
And do the work
To make life sweet
For those who have been so beat.
Remember the nice days.
They're gifts along your way.
Go slowly
And appreciate every day.

For the only measure of me
Is what I think of me,
And I think I'll make it good.

God in Thee

As I traverse this earth,
Whether in my mind or by my feet,
I clearly see the God in thee,
So plainly visible for all to see.

He and she made you and me,
A creation becoming all it can be.
I'm a lesson; you're a lesson,
Blessings on each other's path.

No-one better, no-one righter.
All humble or at least we should be.
Love the only point and purpose.
Forgiveness the only way to free.

Madness, jealousy, greed, our ego.
Destroying this earth, and us as well.
God still hoping his and her created
Find the truth of holy love.

Love is the force that moves our heart.
Love is the breath that fuels our mind.
Love is the food of our highest spirit.
God is the home to which we return.

I pray for all who weep.
I pray for all who sigh.
Until I see you again, my God,
To your creation, fly!

Epilogue

If you liked this collection of poems, thank Emile.
This dear young person told me to keep writing.
She said she thought I was pretty good.
And so I did keep writing.
And I thank her.

Printed in the United States
By Bookmasters